Gluten Free

*The Beginner's Guide to Living the
Gluten-Free Lifestyle Today*

Table of Contents

Introduction

I want to thank you and congratulate you for downloading the book *"**Gluten Free:** The Beginner's Guide to Living the Gluten-Free Lifestyle Today"*.

This book contains proven steps and strategies on how to become a truly, healthy individual away from the perils of the deleterious effects of gluten in the body. People have practically become addicted to gluten, a constituent of wheat, barley, and rye, that they don't even know how harmful and dangerous it is to the body. Some may even be unaware how gluten has inflicted damage to their intestines and many parts of the body. But you know what, there is a solution. This book lays down the secrets to a healthier body without the fear of gluten wrecking havoc on your system.

Here's an inescapable fact: you will need to totally rid your life of gluten to reverse the effects of ingesting that dangerous gluten substance from the time you started eating solid food. You will, however need to adhere to the gluten-lifestyle today. There is not a more opportune time than NOW.

If you do not decide to do it now, it may be too late. You either have gluten sensitivity or not and it will take at least 10 years to diagnose the affliction. Come to think of it, the gluten-free lifestyle benefits your health whether your body is intolerant of gluten or not. So whether by choice or necessity, living gluten-free is a win-win situation. What have you got to lose?

It's time for you to become an amazingly healthy person without the conditions that threaten people for being glued to gluten all their life. Liberate yourself from the bondage of gluten. Embrace the gluten-free lifestyle now. This book tells you how.

Chapter 1

What Is Gluten and Why Is It a Health Threat?

What is Gluten?

Gluten is a key component of cereal grains, functionally classified as storage protein, which is found particularly in barley, rye, and wheat. The sound of the first syllable of the term *gluten* is synonymous to how this component behaves inside the body or as an ingredient in baked food products. When moistened inside the body by digestive juices or in baked food items by other ingredients, it becomes sticky. Thus, foods containing gluten are naturally harder to digest than most other foods. As an ingredient in processed food, gluten helps hold the constituents together.

In wheat flour for example, gluten is used to provide bread dough its desired structure and consistency and its distinctive chewiness. This is why bakers and chefs value gluten in their menu. However, gluten poses a health hazard because it cannot be digested by people with celiac disease or those suffering from gluten intolerance/sensitivity. People are practically clueless about the sudden interest in gluten-free foods. Sudden is, however, not an accurate term for the heightened interest in gluten. This heightened interest is driven by the difficulty of diagnosing gluten sensitivity, which may take about a decade on the average.

If it takes that long to make a correct diagnosis, it is not surprising that many people are gluten-intolerant and may not even know it. And no, this eBook isn't meant to scare you but to keep you well-informed and prevent the hazards that gluten poses on your health. For starters, you can take the short quiz below to gauge the possibility of gluten sensitivity based on the symptoms you experience. Remember, the result of the following quiz is not conclusive, but it offers you some idea to tide you over about some fears you may have felt after reading a few lines about gluten sensitivity.

Quick Quiz on Gluten Sensitivity

Indicate whether or not you experience the following symptoms or if you have been diagnosed with one or more health conditions by marking the appropriate box. There are no correct or incorrect answers.

YES   NO

1. ☐ ☐ Aching joints

2. ☐ ☐ Anemia, particularly, iron deficiency anemia

3. ☐ ☐ Arthritis

4. ☐ ☐ Autoimmune disease (Also, check the yes box if you have a family history of the disease)

5. ☐ ☐ Bloating or gas in your stomach area

6. ☐ ☐ Cancer (Also, check the yes box if you have a family history of cancer)

7. ☐ ☐ Celiac disease (Also, check the yes box if you have a family history of the disease)

8. ☐ ☐ Elimination problems such as constipation or diarrhea

9. ☐ ☐ Fatigue and/or sleeping problems

10. ☐ ☐ Frequent infections or tendency to easily get infections

11. ☐ ☐ Headaches and/or migraine

12. ☐ ☐ Infertility

13. ☐ ☐ Menstrual problems

14. ☐ ☐ Mood swings

15. ☐ ☐ Nausea

16. ☐ ☐ Occasional brief episodes of disorientation lasting just up to a couple of minutes, poor short-term memory, and difficulty in finding the right words (to say) or in substituting words. This is generally called *brain fog*.

17. ☐ ☐ Osteopenia or osteoporosis

18. ☐ ☐ Thyroid disease

19. ☐ ☐ Weight management issues

20. ☐ ☐ Widespread body pain caused by increased sensitivity to pain, together with fatigue, sleeping problems, anxiety, depression, and bladder problems. This is a condition medically described as *fibromyalgia*.

Quick Quiz Interpretation

Count the number of quick quiz items where you answered "YES". A rough interpretation of the possibility that you are gluten-intolerant follows:

Number of Yes Answers	Interpretation
None	Congratulations, you are most probably not suffering from gluten insensitivity, but adhering to a gluten-free diet may work wonders for your health and wellness.
Less than 4	Report for check-up more regularly. Gluten sensitivity may be contributing to your health problems. Also read on for more information about the gluten-free diet.
4 to 7	Request your physician to perform tests to confirm or rule out gluten sensitivity diagnosis. There is a bit of likelihood that you are suffering from it. Also read on for more information about the gluten-free diet.
8 or more	Report for confirmatory gluten sensitivity diagnosis. Change to a gluten-free lifestyle. There is a strong likelihood that you are suffering from it. Also read on for more information about the gluten-free diet.

How Gluten Affects your Health

Without meaning to scare you, gluten affects not just the digestive tract, but other body systems. Directing you back to the quick quiz, only item numbers 2, 5, 10, 15, and 19 are symptoms typical of problems in the digestive system. There is medical evidence that intolerance for gluten also causes symptoms outside of the digestive system. Difficulty in metabolizing this storage protein completely in the intestines may also affect the immune system, the nervous system, and the hormone regulation system. In the United States, three out of 10 people in the population are gluten intolerant but many of them do not exhibit symptoms related to the digestive system.

Quick quiz item numbers 1, 11, 16, and 20 are symptoms that affect the nervous system. Meanwhile, quick quiz item numbers 9, 12, 13, 14, 17, 18, anxiety and depression apart from fibromyalgia are hormone-related symptoms. On the other hand, quick quiz item numbers 3, 4, 6, 7, and 10 are immune system-related symptoms.

The inability of the upper intestines of the digestive tract to completely break down gluten causes the immune system to see the gluten-enzyme combination as a foreign body that the body needs to be defended against. The immune reaction is to get the intestinal wall inflamed. In the ensuing micro-battle, the intestines become 'collateral damage'. With damage inflicted on the intestines, its ability for nutrient absorption is also compromised. This inevitably relaxes the immune defenses due to exhaustion, coupled with deficiencies in vitamins and minerals, and poor nutrition. The weakened immune system is thus unable to provide protection against other gluten-induced health condition in different parts of the body.

Chapter 2

Benefits of a Gluten-Free Lifestyle

Notice that this eBook advocates gluten-free lifestyle, not just gluten-free diet. While preventing the hazards and/or correcting the effects of gluten on your health have a lot to do about food, being gluten free isn't just about your diet. Living a healthy, gluten-free lifestyle is the key to better health and overall wellness.

And your diet is just one aspect of the gluten-free lifestyle. Being gluten-free goes over and above gluten-free grocery list and menus. It spans beyond how you order food when you need to dine out or how you select what to put in your food plate in a social gathering. Believe it or not, how you deal with life's emotional challenges are part of the gluten-free lifestyle.

Additionally, a gluten-free lifestyle isn't just about eliminating gluten from your diet, but more about gaining control of your diet. Gluten is a protein, but since it comes from cereal grains, it goes with carbohydrates. Remember that some carbs are simple sugars. Being gluten-free, therefore, has a lot to do about control over craving for foods containing gluten. A gluten-free lifestyle is, therefore, cannot be a bed of roses especially at the start, but it sure has great health benefits worth all the trouble.

The Joy of Eating Without the Trading-Off your Health

First and foremost among the benefits of gluten-free lifestyle is the chance of discovering more about eating well and eating healthy at the same time. The effects of the changing to a gluten-free lifestyle do not only help you feel better physically, but emotionally as well. Living gluten-free makes sure that what you eat does not harm your body. After all, eating is supposed to nourish your body and to replenish your energy for daily activities, not make you sick.

Efficacy over Chronic Diseases

Being gluten-free decreases the risk of various long-term or chronic health conditions, such as:

- Cardiovascular diseases

- Certain forms of cancer

- Type 2 diabetes

Other Benefits of Being Gluten Free

A gluten-free lifestyle also lowers the incidence of cramps, fatigue and heartburn. It also promotes clearer skin. Gluten-free foods leave out high-fat food items and fried foods, which helps lower serum cholesterol to healthier levels. Additionally people who maintain a gluten-free lifestyle enjoy better digestion and increased body energy for daily activities.

Gluten-free life also promises one with less or no inflammations, since gluten-free foods have anti-inflammatory properties. Being gluten-free empowers your body against germs and viruses as the body's infection-fighting mechanism is enhanced via anti-oxidants. Even healthy individuals, like athletes, can benefit from a gluten-free lifestyle through enhanced performance levels as long as the diet is prepared with ample daily iron requirements.

Chapter 3

Jumping to the Gluten-Free Lifestyle Made Simple

Making a lifestyle change seems to be an overwhelming task. Don't be daunted with the cliché 'No pain, no gain'. The gluten-free lifestyle is not the end of your happy eating days. Rather, it marks the beginning of happier and healthier eating. The gluten-free lifestyle isn't meant to make you live miserably. This eBook can make your transition to a gluten-free lifestyle simpler, so please read on.

The thought of making a lifestyle change may be extremely challenging. Yet, what most people think as an ordeal can be made simple when one embraces the process and subdivides it into an organized set of simple tasks. All you need is to take the first step - have the will to adopt the lifestyle. Here is how you can enjoy a healthy, gluten-free lifestyle.

Before you take the plunge, gluten-free means zero gluten. You don't want to just reduce your gluten intake because it won't work at all. Even if you cut your gluten intake into half, the adverse health effects from the remaining gluten in your diet will just be like you are consuming a gluten-laden diet. The only way to do it is to go gluten-free, which means no gluten at all in your diet.

Get Rid of Gluten in your Kitchen Pantry

Dispose of all types of flour and baking ingredients processed from barley, oats, rye, and wheat. Throw these gluten-containing flours and refrain from giving them away since what is not good for your health is not good for the health of other people too. You may think you are wasting food, but you are doing it for a more important reason - your health. Besides, this is a one-time operation.

Dispose of other ingredients which may not contain gluten but may have been contaminated with gluten when you scooped ingredients like baking powder, baking soda, sugar, salt with a spoon you used to scoop wheat flour while baking or cooking.

Clean your cupboards and drawers. Tidy it for any flour spills and wash all the containers you used very well.

Dispose of all grocery items containing gluten, which may include:

- Canned soups, particularly those labeled as "cream of _____"
  Cereals, cookies, crackers, and pasta processed from durum-wheat, semolina or whole wheat

- Gravy mixes

- Instant noodles and oatmeal

- Other quick-to-prepare and instant foods containing barley, oats, rye, or wheat.

Read the Labels of Food Items Carefully

Not all foods obviously contain gluten. Food product labels do not always scream their ingredients contain gluten. Some may even get away with a gluten-free tag since there is such a thing as unavoidable presence of the ingredient (gluten) at less than 20 parts per million (ppm). To date, what the FDA defines as gluten-free suggests that food items do not contain ingredients that are:

- processed from cereal grains that contain gluten;

- derivatives of cereal grains that contain gluten which have not undergone the process of gluten removal;

- derivatives of cereal grains that contain gluten which have undergone the process of gluten removal, but still contain more than the FDA maximum limit of 20 ppm;

Be on the look-out for masked labels that specify their ingredients indirectly. Some manufacturers call their wheat ingredient as "natural flavors" and the enclose wheat in parentheses. Careless shoppers in search of gluten-free items sometimes fall for this scheme. Some manufacturers list their ingredients straightforward as barley malt, but others attempt to "hide" the barley content of their products by listing malt, malt flavoring or malt vinegar.

Restock your Pantry with Gluten-Free Food and Food Products

The gluten-free food market is an emerging niche. It is, therefore, given that gluten-free foods are a little more expensive, but affordable. The trade-off to consider is to spend your hard-earned dollars on food rather than for the treatment of gluten-induced health conditions. Be ready with your gluten-free shopping list for your next trip to the grocery store. Here is a sample list of gluten-free foods and food products you may include.

Fruits	*Vegetables*	*Dairy Products*
To go easy on your budget, choose the ones in season:	Broccoli	Butter
	Carrots	Cottage cheese
Apples		
	Corn	Cream cheese
Berries		
	Green and red peppers	Cheddar
Cherries		
	Lettuce	Eggs or egg substitute
Grapes		
	Potatoes	Milk
Melon		
	Tomatoes	Mozzarella
Oranges		
		Plain yogurt
Peaches		
		Swiss cheese
Plum		
Canned fruits		
Dried fruits		

Meat and Meat Alternatives	*Grains and Starch*	*Nuts and Seeds*
Beans and peas	Amaranth	Almonds
Fresh beef	Arrowroot	Nut butter from almonds, peanuts or cashew
Fresh fish and shellfish	Brown or white rice	
		Pecans

Fresh poultry (avoid the self-basting types)

Lentils

Buckwheat

Gluten-free millet

Potato starch

Tapioca

Pumpkin seeds

Sesame seeds

Sunflower seeds

Walnuts

Wheat Flour Substitutes

Amaranth flour

Bean flour

Cornstarch

Mesquite flour

Montina flour

Nut flour from almonds, hazelnuts and pecans

Potato flour

Rice flour

Sorghum flour

Soy flour

Miscellaneous

Ensure that you purchase gluten-free items:

Baking soda

Bread/muffin mix

Canola oil

Gluten-free spices and condiments

Olive oil

Pancake or waffle mix

The above list may be modified to suit your specific case. Diabetics, and those who are suffering from other conditions can consult with their dieticians for items which you need to avoid or include in the list.

Chapter 4

The Gluten-Free Psychology Hack: Dealing with your Emotions

There are basically two kinds of people who embark on a gluten-free lifestyle: those who do it by choice or those who do it by necessity. The first team may or may not be a completely healthy group, but having realized the benefits of going gluten-free, they elected to embrace the lifestyle. The latter team is composed of those who need to go gluten-free because they ought to after being diagnosed to have gluten sensitivity or celiac disease. The former have a huge emotional advantage, but both teams may need to deal with the so-called gluten-free blues. Fear not, however, because this chapter presents the gluten-free psychology hack.

From Shock and Panic to Start-up Jitters

Being diagnosed with celiac disease and prescribed a gluten-free lifestyle is not a death sentence but a new lease on life. You have probably been suffering from ailments which doctors cannot diagnose for about a decade or so. Now, you know what is wreaking havoc on your health, you should be more relieved than shocked. You don't even need to undergo a delicate procedure or an experimental treatment, but a lifestyle change. The idea may be quite panicky, though.

Nevertheless, the shock and the panic are normal reactions to the situation. In no time, you will get over that short stage but you could still feel start-up jitters. What are you supposed to eat? Well, your initial shopping list had been prepared in Chapter 3.

Do you need to find special food? There are now a lot of gluten-free foods on the market. But why worry about buying everything when you can easily prepare your own food yourself. Chapter 5 introduces one important facet of the gluten-free lifestyle - the gluten-free diet. Chapter 7 starts you up with easy-to-prepare recipes until you get the hang of it and concoct great gluten-free meals yourself.

Feeling Frustrated and Angry

As you get comfy with the gluten-free diet, there may come a point in time where you get so stressed especially if you have to embrace the gluten-free lifestyle because of a health condition like celiac disease or other forms of gluten sensitivity. There are a host of situations that can make you feel frustrated and angry. Who would want to be handed down a 'defective' system that reacts to gluten in food while other people are not affected? Others feel so frustrated about passing on their gluten intolerance to their children.

Others bear the brunt of choosing gluten-free food products in the supermarket from an avalanche of wheat- and gluten-laden products. Still others get frustrated over the seemingly lukewarm concern of their partners or other household members. Talk it out with the people who can offer you the best support, but deal with it calmly - no lashing out. Anger is a natural emotion but if it gets in the way of your gluten-free lifestyle, it is best to seek professional help.

Dealing with Depression and Grief

If you are used to eating up a lot of gluten in food for decades, switching to a gluten-free lifestyle can be a cause of grief or even trigger depression. The grief is often a case of feeling isolated "from the rest of the world" because you have to stay away from foods that everybody loves. Also, keep in mind that gluten-containing foods are carbs, which you have been ingesting since you were a toddler. You are already addicted to it!

Don't keep your feelings of grief or depression to yourself. The best way is to confide to someone you completely trust. Gluten affects the brain function. If you are already on a gluten-free diet, or you believe you have religiously adhered to a gluten-free lifestyle, consult with a physician. It is also possible that you are ingesting gluten from a nonfood source. This will be discussed on the last part of this chapter.

Dealing with the Blues

At any rate, if your emotional concerns aren't too serious, you can condition your whole body to deal with the gluten-free blues by:

- Avoiding alcohol: Alcohol fuels depression and may cause sleep problems.

- Exercise or physical work-out: Exercise helps fight stress and helps brain production of endorphins, a feel-good natural brain secretion.

- Ensuring a healthy, balanced gluten-free diet: Control your sugar intake, too, because high blood sugar levels adversely affect one's mood.

Beware of Non-Food Gluten-Containing Items

Early on, this book underscored that a gluten-free lifestyle is not just about the food that you consume. When you have embraced the lifestyle for over a year and you are still troubled with the blues, you may be ingesting gluten from a non-food source. Those who are into the gluten-free lifestyle for celiac disease or gluten sensitivity should be wary about these non-edible gluten-containing products. However, those who are in it to stay healthy need not worry much about these non-food gluten sources.

Glues and adhesives are staples in every home for quick-fix tasks on broken items and they contain gluten. There are also non-obvious non-food gluten sources on envelop adhesives, postage stamps, and stickers. Following is a partial list of other non-food sources of gluten in and around the house:

- Art supplies such as clay and Play-Dough, glue, and paste;

- Cleaning agents such as bar soap, dish soap, dishwasher detergent, and soft cleansers;

- Toiletries such as conditioner, facial cleanser, mouthwash, shampoo, and toothpaste;

- Some common beauty products such as lip balm, lipstick, lotion, and sun protection products;

Be careful to use gloves, but those which are not made of latex, which are usually dusted with flour for ease of use. Since household products are not required gluten-free tags, you can contact the manufacturer of products you already have in the house to inquire if their product made use of gluten-containing ingredients. It is your right as a consumer.

Chapter 5

The Gluten-Free Diet Made Simple

Whether you are on the gluten-free diet by choice or by necessity, the gluten-free diet is a very important facet of your new gluten-free lifestyle. Start slow and easy and stay focused on your goal. Remember, your goal is zero gluten, not reduced gluten - it's an "all or nothing" matter. Eliminate all the gluten or else you will derive no benefit at all.

Starting the Gluten-Free Diet

The best way to start the gluten-free diet on your way to a gluten-free lifestyle is to consider a few naturally gluten-free foods and use these in your recipes. Here are some tips to get by:

- Venture to prepare non bread- or flour-based gluten-free dishes.

- Try recipes where any flour can be used.

- Refrain from baking gluten-free bread. Even if you are used to baking, doing it without gluten could be a tricky task and a source of frustration early on.

- There are sumptuous dishes which you may be familiar with that are naturally gluten free, like baked potato and grilled steak. This is provided that diabetes is not among your health conditions and you are allowed to eat a reasonable amount of beef.

- Substitute your usual bread course with vegetables, say garden salad instead of garlic bread.

- Baked ham or roasted chicken served with corn or tapioca are complete meals full of energy and protein sans the harmful gluten.

- Vegetable dishes prepared from the list in Chapter 3 are naturally gluten-free.

Hanging on the Gluten-Free Diet

Once you feel you are getting the hang of the gluten-free diet, you can move on towards a slightly-altered version of your favorite comfort foods. You will be amazed to learn that a lot of standard dishes everybody loves can be made naturally gluten-free. Pasta recipes are all time favorites. You may experiment with different gluten-free pasta goodies until you perfect them to the delight of the whole family. Just remember the following:

- You don't need to change your favorite recipe entirely, just ensure that all your ingredients like sauces and spices are gluten-free.

- Replace your regular pasta noodles with gluten-free noodles.

- If you are using gluten-free pasta noodles for the first time, follow cooking instructions of the pasta as indicated in the package. This applies to all non-gluten containing ingredients you are going to use for the first time.

- Aside from different cooking times, gluten-free pasta derived from corn flour, rice flour or any other flour requires more delicate handling during rinsing when the pasta is cooked. The best move is to read and follow package directions.

- Honestly, pasta noodles sans the gluten content taste differently from the regular wheat-based pasta, but you can compensate for this difference by working on the sauces and the rich, thick aroma. This is what you need to perfect with the gluten-free diet. Once you capture the right taste, even dinner guests wouldn't know they are eating gluten-free pasta.

- If you have the passion for foreign dishes, chicken tacos prepared with corn tortillas, salsa, guacamole, and non-gluten containing fillers will constitute a great treat for the family.

- If you do not have cholesterol issues, you can go and prepare gluten-free Chinese delicacies with rice vermicelli and stir-fried veggies.

Leveling-Up with the Gluten-Free diet

Once you have mastered the art of preparing gluten-free meals, you are ready to expand into more non-gluten-containing meals by substituting with gluten-free products. You are on your way to the more difficult part of going gluten-free: baking without the usual gluten-laden wheat flour:

- Just like when you first started, start baking a few recipes.

- The gluten-free baking challenge for you is to find which non-gluten flour you are most comfortable with. You may choose from the list in Chapter 3 or try other non-gluten flour.

- If you are an experienced baker, cakes make great experiments. Don't worry if your gluten-free cakes turn out not so smooth or even. You can always cover-up the imperfect texture with a generous amount of icing or sprinkles.

Chapter 6

Maintaining Focus: Staying Gluten-Free

The gluten-free lifestyle is not meant to isolate you from the rest of the world. However, social gatherings are not an excuse to munch in some gluten-containing foodies every once in a while. You definitely have a life outside the home as long as you can stay focused on your goal to stay glued to the gluten-free lifestyle.

How to Dine Safely in Restaurants?

Planning and research are the first steps to stay gluten-free even when you need to eat out with family, friends, and colleagues. Search the restaurant website and read on. If you have questions in your mind, obtain their contact details and ask.

For your planning and research to take place, you need to know in advance which restaurant will be the venue of your dinner (or lunch). Never give in to an ambush eat-out invitation even if your friend is paying unless you are sure that the place serves gluten-free meals.

Feel free to communicate your special diet needs to the restaurant and allow enough time for your meal to be prepared to your specifications. Many restaurants are considerate of their client's special diet requirements.

You can call in advance to inquire if the restaurant can address your special diet needs. Otherwise, find another restaurant which can cater to your diet request.

If the restaurant promotes itself as "serving gluten-free delicacies", carefully assess your first experience and provide feedback to management.

Inquire if their food preparation procedures guard against gluten cross contamination. This is an important question to ask the restaurant who may or may not always answer you truthfully. A restaurant that serves gluten-free meals but cannot guarantee cross contamination with gluten-containing substances is not safe for your gluten-free lifestyle.

How to Safely Dine in Non-Restaurant Social Gatherings?

You may call ahead to ask about what foods are going to be served for family gatherings and explain that your gluten-free diet is the reason for asking about the menu in advance.

You may volunteer to bring gluten-free versions of one or two dishes to be served to introduce the non-gluten lifestyle to friends and family.

If you are not sure how the cake served was baked (if it is gluten-free, that is), skip it and go for the ice cream if you don't have trouble with sugar.

Always be ready with gluten-free cookies. They may satisfy your hunger fangs if you are not comfortable whether the foods served are gluten-free. Don't eat party foods unless you are sure they don't contain gluten.

How to Survive Outside the Home without Compromising Your Gluten-Free Lifestyle?

The safest way is to bring packed lunch of gluten-free food to school or to the workplace.

If home-prepared lunch in the office is not a popular culture, research for nearby restaurants which can address your special diet requirements.

You may also communicate your special diet needs to the office cafeteria manager or the catering company servicing your workplace about gluten-free meals.

In the case of children who are also on the gluten-free trail, communicate their special meal requirements in school with the concerned authorities or stick with the packed lunch and snacks routine.

Traveling Gluten-Free

There shouldn't be much challenge about your gluten-free lifestyle when you travel by land or sea if you carry gluten-free food with you.

For longer land or sea trips, consider bringing non-easily perishable gluten-free food or buy your trusted brands during stopovers.

Air travel might be quite cumbersome if you intend to bring gluten-free food. However, in some instances, as long as you comply with the standard airline rules about meals, you need not worry about what to eat.

Global airlines serve special meals to their passengers as long as these are communicated in advance. Make the initiative to work for the special meal arrangements.

Chapter 7

Bonus Chapter: Sample Gluten-Free Recipes for Breakfast, Lunch and Dinner

Try the following gluten-free recipes for breakfast, lunch, and dinner. Start the day guilt free, surprise your gustatory sense at mid-day and cap your day with an easy-to-prepare touch of the Orient. You can also use these recipes as examples. Complement these recipes with some great ingredient substitution experiments and in no time, you will have compiled an awesome database of gluten-free treats for family, friends, and colleagues.

Breakfast

Guiltless French-Toast with Syrup

Number of Servings: 4

Ingredients for the Toast	Ingredients for the Syrup
1 tablespoon (tbsp) honey	1 tbsp honey
1 teaspoon (tsp) vanilla	1 tsp cornstarch
¼ tsp cinnamon	½ cup freshly squeezed orange juice
¼ tsp nutmeg	½ tsp orange zest
2 cups gluten-free, casein-free (GFCF) non-dairy milk	¼ teaspoon cinnamon
4 pieces (pcs) eggs or egg substitute	
8 slices GFCF bread	

GFCF oil	

Procedure:

1. Spray the baking dish with GFCF oil and arrange the 8 bread slices in 2 overlapping rows.

2. Mix the eggs or egg substitute, cinnamon, honey, non-dairy milk, nutmeg, and vanilla and whisk the ingredients until well-blended.

3. Pour the blended egg mixture over the bread slices. Cover the dish and put inside the refrigerator for at least 1 hour before cooking or overnight.

4. After an hour of refrigeration or in the morning, cook the bread covered in the egg mixture for 40 minutes at 350 degrees or until puffed and light golden in color.

5. Combine all the syrup ingredients in a saucepan. Cook at medium heat and stir constantly until thick and boiling. If you have a desired syrup consistency, you opt to add more orange juice.

6. Serve the baked toast with the orange syrup.

Lunch

Chicken Peach Surprise

Number of Servings: 4

Ingredients for the Chicken	Ingredients for the Sauce
1 tsp sage (dried)	1 jar peach jam (in sweetened fruit juice)
1 tsp thyme (dried)	1 tbsp lemon juice or lime juice

½ cup vegetable oil	1 tsp horseradish
½ tsp ground pepper (freshly-ground)	
½ tsp paprika	
½ tsp salt	
2 pounds chicken breasts (boneless, skinless)	
2 tsp GF flour	
3 cups GF rice cereal (unsweetened)	

Procedure:

1. Prepare oven for preheating at 400 degrees.

2. Use a food processor or blender to mix the following ingredients for the crumb mixture: cereal, flour, paprika, pepper, sage, salt, and thyme. Put in a bowl when mixed.

3. Cut the chicken into desired size.

4. Place oil in shallow bowl and dip chicken into the oil. Afterwards, dip chicken into the crumb mixture.

5. Line a baking pan in aluminum foil, spray with oil, and arrange the chicken in the pan. Put all the remaining oil into the baking pan and bake in the preheated oven for 20 minutes or until cooked and tender.

6. Soften the peach jam by putting it into the microwave for about 2 minutes.

7. Mix jam with the lime juice and horseradish. The mixture is served as a dipping sauce. To enhance the flavor of the recipe, GF barbeque sauce, ketchup and honey may be added to the dipping sauce if desired.

Dinner

Oriental Penne Salad

Number of Servings: 6 to 8

Ingredients for the Pasta	Ingredients for the Vinaigrette
1 bunch sliced green onions	1 tbsp GF soy sauce
1 cup bean sprouts	½ five-spice Chinese seasoning
1 cup broccoli, cut as desired	½ teaspoon salt
1 cup chopped carrots	2 cloves minced garlic
½ cup pea pods, cut as desired	2 tbsp red wine
½ pound rice penne	6 tbsp olive oil
2 tbsp minced ginger root (fresh)	

Procedure:

1. Cook the penne pasta as per package directions, rinse in cold water when cooked, and drain well.

2. Mix the pasta ingredients and the vinaigrette in separate bowls.

3. Serve the cooked pasta with the ingredients and the vinaigrette.

Conclusion

Thank you again for downloading this book!

I hope this book was able to help you to realize the health benefits of a gluten-free lifestyle. Whether you take the plunge to the gluten-free lifestyle by choice or by necessity, you are on your way to a healthier body and a sound mind. Remember how gluten affects your mood!

The next step is to apply the new knowledge you gained and live gluten-free. You have nothing to lose but your gluten. But you have a full life ahead to enjoy, free from sickness and worries of failing health.

Finally, if you enjoyed this book, please take the time to share your thoughts and post a review on Amazon. It'd be greatly appreciated!

Thank you and good luck!

Preview of 'Water Diet'
A Proven Diet for Losing Weight, Having More Energy and Speeding Up your Metabolism Today

Chapter 1: Benefits of Drinking Water

Water is very essential. Without water, you will not be able to continue living. In fact, you need to drink several glasses a day in order to keep your body hydrated and healthy. Water is generally present in the food and liquids you intake. It is necessary to replace the amounts of water that you lose each day. Fluid losses actually occur continuously in the form of urine, stool and sweat. In order for your body to stay functional, you need to have these fluids replaced by drinking sufficient amounts of water.

What's more, there are plenty of other reasons why you should drink water. For instance, water can help maintain the balance of fluids in your body. As you know, your body is made up of sixty percent water, and the fluids in your body are responsible for absorption, digestion, circulation, saliva production, body temperature maintenance and nutrient transportation. Your brain and your kidneys communicate with each other to know how much water your body has to excrete in the form of urine.

When your body becomes low on water or fluids, your brain triggers your thirst mechanism. This makes you thirsty, unless you are on certain medications that make you want to drink. However, when you get thirsty, see to it that you drink anything except alcohol. You can have water, milk or juice but not alcoholic beverages. Alcohol can interfere with the communication between your brain and kidneys, thus, excreting more fluids than necessary. This can make you dehydrated.

Another reason why you should drink water is because it can help you control your calories and manage your weight. In fact, dieters have resorted to drinking a lot of water to lose weight for years. Although water does not contain any weight loss properties, it can help lose weight if you choose it over beverages with higher calories. For instance, instead of drinking canned juices or soda, you can simply drink water. If you do this habitually, you will soon notice weight loss.

Likewise, foods that have high water content can help you feel like fuller longer. Hence, you will not feel hungry all the time. You will no longer crave for snacks in the middle of the day or night. You may not even be hungry for desserts. When you eat less frequently, you will be able to shed off those excess pounds. Fruits, vegetables, beans, broth-based soups and oatmeal are example of foods that have high water content. They tend to require more chewing and they are absorbed more slowly by your body.

In addition, drinking water can give you energy. Yes, water can indeed help energize your muscles. If your body lacks water, your cells will not be able to maintain their balance of electrolytes and fluids. As a result, you will become tired more easily. If your muscles do not receive sufficient amounts of fluids, they will not be able to function properly. This will prevent you from completing your tasks quickly and efficiently. You will easily get tired after doing simple activities.

Of course, you need to drink sufficient amounts of water when you exercise. The American College of Sports Medicine has released guidelines for exercisers to follow. These guidelines include information regarding the amount of fluid that you have to intake before and during your exercise routine. Ideally, you should consume about seventeen ounces of fluid a couple of hours before you start to exercise. You should also drink fluids at regular intervals during your exercise.

Dehydration can cause a reduction in your blood volume. This can lead to a reduction in oxygen supply to your muscles. In turn, this can lead to tiredness and exhaustion. If your muscles do not receive adequate oxygen supply, your body will get tired more easily and quickly. Also, you should take note that calorie burning requires water supply. If you are dehydrated, you will not be able to burn off fats. Calorie burning also produces toxins, and you need water to get these toxins out of your body.

Drinking water regularly is also good for your skin. Just like any other part of your body, your skin needs water to stay in top shape. Your skin has a protective barrier that helps prevent too much loss of fluid. You can drink water to hydrate your skin and prevent dryness and wrinkles. Your kidneys will excrete the excess fluids once you are hydrated adequately. If you want to lock in moisture, you can choose a moisturizer. It will create a physical barrier to prevent the moisture from escaping your skin.

Water is good for your kidneys, and your kidneys are very important organs in your body. Your body fluids carry waste products to and from cells, with the most major toxin being blood urea nitrogen. It is actually a water-soluble waste that passes through your kidneys and excreted in your urine. Your kidneys cleanse your body of toxins, so make sure to drink sufficient amounts of fluid. You can say that you are properly hydrated if your urine is odorless and light in color.

On the other hand, you are not properly hydrated if your urine does not flow freely, has an odor and is concentrated. Your kidneys store extra fluids for your bodily functions, which is why the color, odor and concentration of your urine increase if you do not drink sufficient amounts of fluid. If you habitually drink very little water or fluid, then your risk of having kidney stones may be higher. This is especially true if you live in a place with a warm climate.

Moreover, drinking water on a regular basis can help you manage your bowel movements more easily. When you are adequately hydrated, your gastrointestinal tract will function properly and prevent you from having constipation. On the other hand, if you do not drink enough water, your colon will pull water from your stools so your body can stay hydrated. If this happens, you will be constipated. Hence, you should make it a habit to drink sufficient amounts of water as well as eat foods that are rich in fiber.

Fiber is good for digestion. You can get fiber from vegetables and whole wheat. However, fiber alone cannot flush out the toxins from your body. Without sufficient fluids, it can actually cause constipation instead of ridding your body of toxins. Water also helps keep your muscles toned by helping them contract as well as lubricate your joints. You can avoid having sore joints and muscles when you exercise if you are properly hydrated.

Anyway, if you think that you are not getting enough fluids, you should make it a habit to drink something each time you have a meal or a snack. Again, you can drink juices, milk or water but you should stay away from alcoholic beverages as much as possible. Likewise, you should avoid drinking caffeinated beverages such as soda, coffee and tea. These are diuretics and they can cause your body to excrete water. In case you drink a diuretic, make sure that you think enough water to compensate.

If you have an alcoholic drink, do not forget to drink water with it. You should also drink water before and after you have this alcoholic beverage in order to prevent tiredness and hangover headache. If you are bored with drinking plain water, you can add a few drops of lemon to give it favor. Also, you should opt for freshly squeezed juices instead of canned ones. Canned beverages are usually full of sugars and preservatives.

If you are watching calories, you can have non-caloric drinks aside from water. If you have a hectic schedule, make it a point to have a bottle of water inside your bag, desk or car. Drink a glass of water as soon as you wake up. You should also make it a habit to eat vegetables and fruits, especially the ones that have high water content. Take note that about twenty percent of your fluid intake comes from the food you eat. So, you should always watch and what you eat. Avoid salty, sugary and artificially flavored foods.

If you enjoy this preview, then *click here for the full story of this eBook!* Or go to: *http://www.amazon.com/dp/B00JNSNS04/*

Kindly Check My Other Works!

Hereunder, you will find a few of my eBooks that are presently live at Amazon. Just click the following Title Links to check them out, to wit;

- *The Illuminati Secrets Exposed: Learn the Secrets of the Illuminati and What You Can Do to Set Yourself Free*

- *Spirit Guides: Learn How to Contact your Spiritual Guides and Travel the Spiritual Plane Today*

- *How to Braid Hair: The Complete Guide to Braiding Hair in All the Most Popular Styles Today*

- *Astral Projection: Proven Techniques and Methods for Learning to Travel Astral Plain*

- *Habit Stacking: The Small Changes that Make a Big Difference*

- *Nikola Tesla: The Imagination and Man that Invented the World as We Know It Today*

If the links do not work for whatever reasons, simply search for those titles on the Amazon to find them.

Other free eBook are now available, *click here for your subscription!*

Free eBooks!

Thanks for reading! Below you'll find a link to your free eBook download of

"HOW TO BE SUCCESSFUL IN LIFE"

Click Here